The School of St Helen +
Abingdon
Berks.

H.D. 73.

# BRITAIN IN PICTURES
## THE BRITISH PEOPLE IN PICTURES

---

# BRITISH MERCHANT ADVENTURERS

GENERAL EDITOR

W. J. TURNER

*

The Editor is most grateful to all those who have
so kindly helped in the selection of illustrations,
especially to officials of the various public
Museums, Libraries and Galleries, and
to all others who have generously
allowed pictures and MSS.
to be reproduced.

# BRITISH
# MERCHANT ADVENTURERS

## MAURICE COLLIS

*WITH*
*8 PLATES IN COLOUR*
*AND*
*24 ILLUSTRATIONS IN*
*BLACK & WHITE*

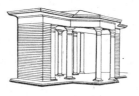

WILLIAM COLLINS OF LONDON
MCMXXXXII

PRODUCED BY
ADPRINT LIMITED LONDON

*

PRINTED
IN GREAT BRITAIN
BY WILLIAM BROWN AND CO. LTD. LONDON

FORT WILLIAM, CALCUTTA IN THE KINGDOM OF BENGAL
Built for the East India Company of England
Engraving from the London Magazine, 1754

# LIST OF ILLUSTRATIONS

## *PLATES IN COLOUR*

THE MARKET PLACE AT GOA IN THE 16TH CENTURY
Engraving from Linschoten's *Itinerario* 1579-1592

# FOREWORD

NO satisfactory explanation has ever been given of the astonishing expansion of British power overseas which began immediately after the English succeeded in preventing the Spaniards from invading this country, then a poor and sparsely populated island with little standing among the kingdoms of the world.

What was the secret of this extraordinary expansion and how was it that so small a maritime power, one of the smallest in Europe, grew into the vast empire which has since become something entirely new in history—namely, a Commonwealth of Nations?

The answer is that this amazing development was largely due to individuals and was not state-planned, as were the empires of Spain and Portugal, which did not endure. Private enterprise, courage and audacity founded the British Empire and it owes its persistence into the present more to men than to policy. The object of this short book is to show some of the ways in which this expansion took place by sketching the lives of six remarkable men, each of whom typifies in his career the adventurous genius of the British race.

EDITOR.

## CHAPTER ONE

# RALPH FITCH: MERCHANT TRAVELLER
## (*fl* 1583–1611)

W HEN Queen Elizabeth came to the throne in 1558, her dominion extended only over England and Ireland. Her subjects were few, poor, and backward, and were in grave danger of being subjugated by Spain. But for a reason no one can entirely explain, they were animated by a spirit for which there was no warrant in the size of their territory and their reasonable prospects. This spirit was a compound of pride, love of liberty, and resolution. They were quite sure they could do as well as or better than the great states of the continent. The Portuguese and the Spaniards during the previous half century had discovered Asia and the Americas, and with the Pope's sanction had divided between them the vast trade of these continents. These discoveries had enormously enriched them, and Spain planned to found a united Catholic order in Europe under her king. But the idea of Spain ruling the world seemed nonsense to the English because man for man they felt themselves superior to the Spaniards. In riches and possessions, however, they were a long way behind them. The realization of all this, and the determination to change it, caused an uprush of the national genius, which showed itself in every department of life. The government was inclined to lag, to talk of prudence. Elizabeth was a very cautious woman. Philip II's power was formidable on paper. But the people wanted fighting and adventures. Without the Queen's sanction, many privateers were fitted out and preyed on the Spanish trading galleons. Drake was the most famous of such buccaneers. He sailed round the world in a ship the size of a small schooner, arriving home with half a million pounds worth of loot, as much as the whole revenue of the Crown for a year.

But this was not business and the merchants of London and other cities, some of whom had long been combined for trade in Europe under the name of the Merchant Adventurers of England, were very desirous of straightforward settled trade with the East. In the twenty-third year of the reign they resolved to send out men to report on what could be bought and what sold in Asia. These travellers were to go via Syria and the Persian Gulf, because the Portuguese, who, in the division, had taken the Eastern trade and used the Cape route, would have tried to sink intruders who went that way. Moreover, in 1580, Portugal had been united to Spain the arch-enemy of England, and Spain's enemies were now Portugal's.

JAHANGIR DRINKING WINE UNDER A CANOPY

Indian painting by Manohar

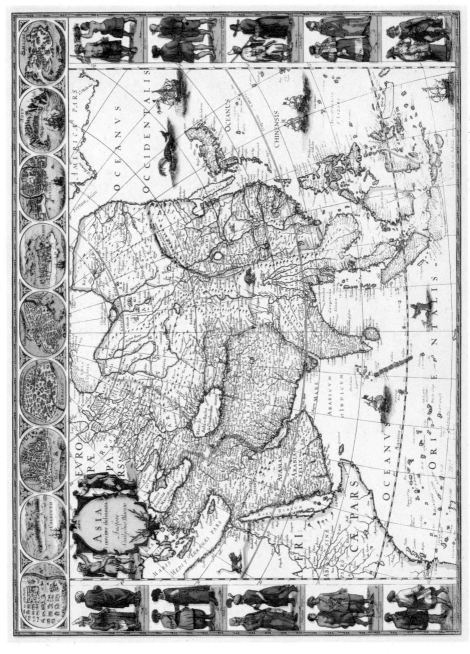

MAP OF ASIA BY J. BLAEU, 1632

PORTRAIT OF AKBAR
Indian drawing of the late 16th century

So in February, 1583, a party of merchant-travellers set out. They were financed by a particular syndicate called the Turkey Company which was backed by a charter from Queen Elizabeth. Among them was Ralph Fitch of London. " Her husband's to Aleppo gone, master of the Tiger," says the First Witch in Macbeth, and it was to that identical place they first went and on that very ship. Travelling thence overland they came to Basra, at the head of the Persian Gulf. Some of the merchants remained there, but Fitch and three others were deputed to proceed to India. They had a letter from Elizabeth addressed to Akbar, the Great Mughal. But at Ormuz, an island at the mouth of the Gulf, from which they planned to slip across the Arabian Sea, they were arrested by the Portuguese, who had a fortress there.

The charge was heresy, but the reason, of course, trade jealousy : the Portuguese knew the English had come to make enquiries. So as heretics they were sent prisoners to Goa, the capital of the Portuguese Indies, where an Inquisition existed and a Grand Inquisitor. This Inquisition was notoriously severe, more cruel and terrifying than the Inquisition of Spain.

Besides the prison of the Inquisition, there were two other notorious prisons in Goa known as the Salle and the Al Jabir. It was in one or other of these that Fitch and his three companions were confined. Both were filthy underground dungeons in which galley-slaves and common malefactors of all races were crowded together, in stifling heat and without sanitation. Bad as English prisons were at that time they were pleasant places in comparison.

B

Joannes à Doetechum fecit.

| | | |
|---|---|---|
| Provinciæ Pegu incola, auri adamantum et rubineorum feraæ, undelacca sigillatoria advehitur. | Incola ex Insulis Moluco, ubi Caryophylla magnâ copiâ crescunt, quorum vestes e stramnt sunt factæ | Penequais familiæ, a Divo Thoma execratæ, intotam (ut Indi referunt) pro-geniem |
| Een uut Pegu, waer veel gout diamanten en robynen gevonden en het negellack, gemaeckt woert | Een inwoonder uut die Eylanden van Moluco, daer die Garyophyl. ngelen overvloedich groyen, welcks cleeren van stroy zyn. | Van penekays gheslachten van S. Thomas als die Indianen seggen gantselicken vervloeckt. 64 en 65 |

THE INHABITANTS OF PEGU AND THE MOLUCCAS
Engraving from Linschoten's *Itinerario*, 1579-1592

But by good fortune a member of the Jesuit College at Goa happened to be an Englishman. This was Father Stevens, the first of this nation known to have set foot in India. Thanks to him, they were released on bail after a month and took a house in the city.

The Goa they saw was at the height of its prosperity. It was the most beautiful city which any Western nation has ever built in the East. The palaces and churches were in Spanish baroque. As admirable as any in that style in Europe, they seemed more enchanting set in a tropic landscape. Gorgeously dressed, the Portuguese, both high and low, attended by Indian or African slaves, paraded the main streets, saluting each other with the extravagance of actors in melodrama. The shops were packed with all the products of the East. Fitch noted the luxury and splendour, little dreaming that one day his countrymen would build greater (though less beautiful) Indian cities. After five months, no further proceedings having been taken against them,

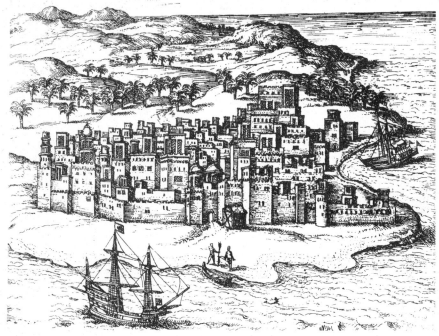

VIEW OF ORMUZ

Engraving from H. Braun's *Civitates Orbis Terrarum*, 1588-1594

the Englishmen asked for the return of their bail money. " The Viceroy made a very sharp answer," writes Fitch in the narrative of his travels, " and sayd wee should be better sifted before it were long, and that they had further matter against us." This alarmed them and when they heard privately that they were to be given the strappado, a torture where you were hoisted by ropes tied to the wrists and then suddenly dropped a distance so as to dislocate the arms, they fled secretly one early morning. Travelling across the continent they made their way to Fatehpur Sikri, the wonderful red sandstone city which Akbar had just built. There they saw the Mughal Court at its greatest moment, but were not given formal audience by the Emperor and so were unable to deliver Queen Elizabeth's letter. Probably as mere travelling merchants they were not qualified for that honour. Moreover, they had no presents. Nevertheless, one of them, Leeds, a jeweller, was given employment at Court on a good salary.

It was at this point that Fitch decided to undertake the journey on which his fame rests. He would go to Burma. No Englishman, as far as is recorded, had ever been to that country. Parts of it were well known to Portuguese adventurers, free-lances and mercenaries who sold their services, often as artillerymen, to the Burmese Kings. Two Italian travellers, Frederici and Balbi, had visited Pegu, the capital, and published memoirs. But it may safely be said that very few people in England knew anything of the kingdom, nearly twice as large as France, which lay between India and China.

In September, 1584, Fitch started alone. Taking boat on the Ganges he floated down to Hugli in Bengal, a Portuguese settlement independent of the Viceroy of Goa, situated near the site of the present city of Calcutta, noting as he went the products of the countryside. From Hugli he passed into Chittagong, where, embarking on a Portuguese ship—the Portuguese here were more buccaneers than merchants—he sailed along the coast of the Bay of Bengal till he reached one of the mouths of the Irrawaddy. Ascending that river to Bassein he transferred to a small boat and in ten days came by tidal riverways to Pegu.

For an Elizabethan, Burma was a strange, incomprehensible place. The Mohamedan and Hindu religions of India were understood to the extent that the followers of the first were called Moors and of the second Gentiles. But no European could have said more of the Buddhism of Burma than that it was a kind of paganism. A great deal of what Fitch saw was, therefore, wholly unintelligible to him. He had not the smallest notion of Burmese history. The reigning king was styled Nanda Bayin, the son of Bayin Naung, whom the Portuguese called Braginoco, as if he were some paynim knight in Ariosto. And indeed he had been a galloping high-coloured personage who had united all Burma and conquered Siam. He died at sixty-six, leaving ninety-seven children. By him was laid out on a grand scale a new city of Pegu, which was filled with the loot he had taken from Siam. There his son, Nanda Bayin, now sat, the most important monarch in all the territories which lay between the domain of Akbar and of Wan Li, the Son of Heaven. But neither of these two Emperors, particularly the latter, would have admitted him to be more than a barbarian.

For Fitch, however, he was a great king. Pegu was so much bigger than London. " Pegu is a citie very great, strong and fair," he writes, " and very populous, and is made square and with very faire walles, and a great ditch round about it full of water, with many crocodiles in it. It hath twenty gates. The streets are the fairest that ever I saw, as straight as a line from one gate to the other, and so broad that tenne or twelve men may ride a front thorow them. The king's house is in the middle of the city," he goes on, and describes

AN INQUISITION SCENE AT GOA IN THE 17TH CENTURY
Engraving from Dellon's *Relations de l'Inquisition de Goa*, 1688

a wooden palace, gilded and carved, before the gate of which were the elephant stables, where stood hundreds of black and four white elephants.

These particular white elephants were the most valuable part of the loot taken by the king's father, Bayin Naung, from Siam. At different periods in the world's history different things are valued and for different reasons. In sixteenth century Burma the four white elephants were worth so much that not all the wealth of the country could have bought them. The only other comparable object in Pegu was a tooth of the Buddha, which had been procured by treaty from Ceylon. But here some doubt existed, for the Viceroy of Goa declared that he and the Archbishop had destroyed the veritable tooth when

THE WHITE ELEPHANT OUTSIDE THE PALACE AT AMARAPURA
Capital of Burma in the early 19th Century
Lithograph from Yule's *Mission to the Court of Ava*, 1855

it fell into Portuguese hands after a battle. They had done so because they believed it to be a potent relic of the Devil.

Fitch went to see the white elephants. Visitors were allowed in on payment of half a ducat. He saw their gilded stable and watched them eat from gold plate. He also watched them having a bath in the river. As they walked to the bank, their attendants shading them from the sun with parasols, a band played ; and when they came out of the water there was a gentleman in court robes ready with a silver basin to wash the mud off their feet. Fitch saw all this, but he did not know that they treated the white elephants in this way because of the belief that the soul of a future World saviour in its long upward transmigration was lodging in each animal. As to black elephants, there were thousands of them trained for battle, in which they played the part of tanks in modern warfare.

Fitch did not aspire to be received by Nanda Bayin, but he saw him giving audience attended by his *She-min* or Ministers and saw petitioners *ski-ko*, a prostration very similar to the Chinese kotow. He also saw the King riding abroad " with a great guard and many noblemen," sometimes on an elephant, at others in a palanquin. And he heard of his great treasure of rubies, sapphires and spinels. Yet he perceived his weakness : " This king hath little force by sea, because he hath but very few ships." That was the mortal weakness which eventually was the ruin of Burma. Fitch's real business, however, was to observe the trade, and in his account he gives a list of the chief commodities as well as the foreign goods for which there was demand.

After visiting Rangoon and the Shwe-dagon pagoda—his description of the latter might stand for it today—he left Pegu for Chiengmai in Northern Siam, never dreaming that one day the capital where he had seen such riches and state would be a country town administered by an English official. The writer of this book has often been there, seen the remnant of the great walls and the crocodile moat.

When he had investigated the trade at Chiengmai he returned to Pegu and took ship to Malacca near Singapore, where the Portuguese had a fortress which commanded the straits. On the way he passed Martaban, Tavoy, Mergui and Junkseylon, palm-fringed little ports where the wind always blows, in one of which, Mergui, a hundred years later so many Englishmen were to be massacred, as will be related in Chapter III. Having noted the vital importance of the Straits of Malacca for a maritime power trading to the Far East, he returned to Pegu and at last set his face for home, travelling by sea to Ceylon, thence up the West Coast of India to Cochin, then to Goa, where he was careful only to remain three days, and so on to Basra, Babylon, Mosul, Aleppo and " by God's assistance safely to London."

He had been away eight years and except for his narrow escape at Goa had had no misadventures. He had travelled some twenty-four thousand miles by sea and land, mostly alone and at a period when travelling of the kind was extremely dangerous, yet he was neither robbed nor shipwrecked. He had acquired a mass of firsthand information of the greatest importance, which, when it was sifted by the merchants of London, led to the founding nine years later of the East India Company, the great organization which in the course of two hundred and fifty years was to acquire for England almost all the towns he had visited. In 1611 he died and is buried in St. Catherine Cree in Leadenhall Street, a most remarkable man, hardly known because what he accomplished was more solid than brilliant ; because he was overshadowed by the many dramatic figures of the Elizabethan era ; and because the little he wrote of himself and his travels was modestly worded and hardly hinted at the multitudinous perils through which he had passed unhurt.

## CHAPTER TWO

# SIR THOMAS ROE : MERCHANT-AMBASSADOR
## (1580-1644)

THE East India Company was a monopoly. By the Royal Charter of 1601, the right to trade in the Eastern seas was reserved to its shareholders. At the time monopolies were a normal way of encouraging trade, though there were plenty of men to say that an Englishman had an inherent right to trade freely wherever he liked. But it was reasonably contended for the monopoly of the Eastern trade that only a body which had not to face competition and was protected by the Crown could hope to pay its way in the face of the dangers and obstacles inherent in an attempt to force English trade in the face of Portuguese opposition.

The first ship sent by the Company to India did not arrive there until 1608. It was commanded by William Hawkins and put into Surat, the chief western port of the Mughal's dominion. Hawkins journeyed to Agra, the Imperial capital, to solicit permission to open trade, Jahangir having recently succeeded his father, Akbar. He remained in Agra for three years. The Emperor granted leave to trade at Surat, but the Portuguese, who were strongly represented at Court by Jesuits, succeeded in obtaining the cancellation of this grant and the virtual expulsion of Hawkins in 1611.

The Company tried again. In 1612 Thomas Best managed to come to an agreement with the imperial officials at Surat. But it was a very limited and insecure arrangement. The Company wanted a charter of rights from the Emperor himself which would place English commerce on a firm and enduring basis. To effect this the Jesuit diplomats at the Court of Agra must be confronted by an English diplomat as clever as themselves. Accordingly it was decided to send, with King James's sanction and credence, an ambassador to Jahangir.

For this entirely novel and most difficult appointment the Company selected in 1614 Sir Thomas Roe, a man of thirty-four years of age, who was a Member of Parliament and had made a voyage of discovery to South America. His grandfather had been Lord Mayor of London. The plan was for him to go to the Indian capital, take up his residence there, get the better of the Portuguese Jesuits and foster and expand the trade which had been tentatively begun. James gave him a letter addressed to Jahangir. He was to press for a treaty of free trade between the two countries. It was known that the Court of India was a splendid court and that to impress it Roe would require money and presents. But the Company was not in a position to do very much.

SIR THOMAS ROE
Engraving by Vertue after Miereveldt

His salary was fixed at £600 a year, a sum equal to at least £5,000 nowadays, but the incomes of the big people at Jahangir's Court ran into tens or even hundreds of thousands. Moreover, his staff was not very brilliant. A chaplain and a doctor on £50 and £24 per annum were supplied, Roe himself having to pay the wages of the rest of his retinue from an annual grant of £100. Later he records in his diary how ashamed he was of his clothes. The Mughals were dressed in the most dazzling manner. " Five years allowance would not have furnished me with one indifferent suit sortable to theirs," he writes. But important though clothes and presents were at the Court of India, they were not everything. Intelligence, firmness, courage, an engaging address, had their effect there as everywhere else. And Roe was a very intelligent man, of indomitable courage, with great charm of manner. Anthony à Wood calls

17

him a scholar and a gentleman. But he was also a very subtle man of affairs. He arrived at Surat in September, 1615.

The Mughal dominion in India was analogous to the Mongol dominion which Marco Polo saw in China three hundred years before. In both cases Nomad horsemen of Mongolian type inhabiting the vast steppe between Manchuria and the Caspian had left their pastures and taken possession of an old agricultural empire. The nomads of Genghis and Kubilai were largely barbarians, and the Chinese civilized them. The Mughals, however, had acquired a tincture of Persian Moslem culture before they entered India. There were, moreover, already Indian Moslem states, for similar nomads had been raiding the sub-continent for six centuries. The Mughals conquered these as well as the Hindus, the inhabitants proper of the country, whom they were careful to leave in the enjoyment of their religion and customs. The Court itself was a sort of colonial version of the Court of Persia ; the tone was nominally Moslem but in reality sceptic, and its literature, painting, calligraphy and ceremonial were derived wholly from Persian models. Besides art, sport held an important place, hunting, shooting, hawking and polo being considered the proper relaxations of a gentleman. The women had lost the freedom of the steppe and were confined in harems guarded by eunuchs. Brahmanical India went its own way outside. There were Hindus, however, in the civil service, and there were Hindu women in the imperial seraglio. As Jahangir's mother was a Rajput, he was half Hindu. His father, Akbar's, mother had been Persian. Thus the original nomad blood in the royal house was much diluted. Educated though the Court was, its information was limited. It did not realize that Europe, though poor and backward in many ways, had recently made scientific discoveries of great promise. Nor had it a proper conception of the new importance of sea power. But in these respects it did not differ from the far grander and more sophisticated Court of China.

Roe had not a good reception at Surat. The Governor, a man called Zulfikar Khan, was a nominee of Prince Khurram, Jahangir's favourite son and the future Emperor. This prince, with Jahangir's Empress, the famous Nur Mahal, one of the most remarkable women in Indian history, was the head of the Court faction which favoured the Portuguese. Zulfikar Khan, therefore, made difficulties when Roe announced that he desired to proceed to the capital. However, the Emperor, on learning that an ambassador from the King of England had come with new presents—Jahangir had a mania for novelties— gave orders for him to be sent up. The Court was then at Ajmere, two months' journey inland. Roe arrived there on 13 December, 1615, having met en route that astonishing eccentric, Tom Coryat, a London writer, who had walked to India as a diversion !

REPUTED PORTRAIT OF NUR JAHAN, WIFE OF JAHANGIR
From a Manuscript in the Bodleian Library

Roe had decided on the line he should take. He must stand on his dignity as an ambassador, refuse to bend, refuse to bribe, show that an envoy of his rank was very different from Fitch and Hawkins, put his case with patience, expound the advantages of trade with England, declare there was plenty of room for both English and Portuguese, and work so that reason and common sense should prevail. It was from Portuguese animosity that he had most to fear. But he was fortified by the reflection that Portugal's position in Eastern waters was not so strong as it had been. If it came to a fight, he knew the British could beat her armadas. The Dutch had recently appeared in Indian seas and were also bent on breaking her monopoly. But Roe did not want it to come to a fight. That would annoy the Mughal and, moreover, cause such expenditure that the trade would pay no dividends for years. If humanly possible he must carry through his mission by diplomacy.

On 10 January he was received in audience by Jahangir. The Emperor sat in a gallery overlooking a wide courtyard full of people. Roe was conducted through the crowd to a rail enclosing a space for men of a better class, where he made a reverence towards the Emperor in the English Court manner. Thereupon he was led across this first enclosure into a second, which was raised somewhat and well carpeted. This was full of courtiers and men of quality. Here he made a reverence again and was taken on until he stood immediately below the balcony, not a high one, on which Jahangir was seated. As he made his third reverence, sweeping the carpet with the plume of his hat, the Emperor bade him welcome with pleasant informality. Roe thereupon handed up King James's letter and some presents. Jahangir seemed very pleased. He talked affably through an interpreter, enquiring after Roe's health, which had not been good, and offering to send him his own physician. No business was discussed. At the end of the audience Roe was congratulated by some of those present on his reception, which had been, they said, more gracious than any accorded to ambassadors from Turkey or Persia.

But he was a very long way from obtaining his desires. The clique headed by the Empress and the Heir-Apparent was by no means pleased that the Emperor had received him. He himself did not understand at that time the composition of the Court parties, and was more optimistic than the real facts warranted. Jahangir's affability had less importance than appeared because Nur Mahal dominated her husband. Moreover, Jahangir did not regard him as an ambassador from a monarch of equal rank. He considered King James no more than the petty king of a remote island.

Among the presents were a coach, a virginal and a sword. Jahangir had asked Roe's musician, Thomas Armstrong, to play on the virginal there and then and was so intrigued by the music that he took him into his employ. From where he sat he could not see the coach well, for it was outside the courtyard, but that evening he went down and got into it and commanded his men to draw him about. Later, at ten o'clock at night, he sent for Roe to show him how the sword should be worn, and " marched up and downe, draweing yt and flourishing." Jahangir was nearly always drunk by 10 p.m.

For the next week or so Roe remained at his lodging, for the fever he had caught returned. He was homesick and low, and felt a strong distaste for the people with whom he would have to negotiate. Writing to his friend, Lord Carew, on the 17th, he said: " This is the dullest basest place that ever I saw."

On the 24th, restored to health and spirits, he attended the Emperor's Durbar, as the levee held from the balcony was called. When Jahangir caught

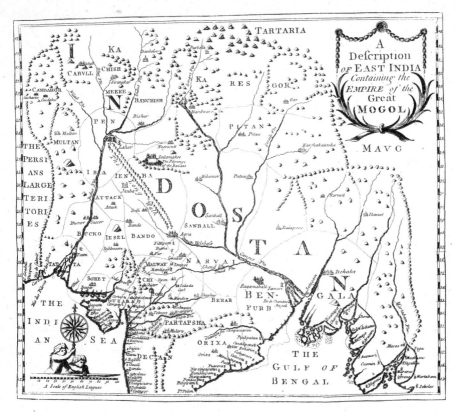

A MAP OF THE TERRITORIES OF THE GREAT MUGHAL CONTEMPORARY WITH ROE
Engraving from Edward Terry's *Voyage to East India*, 1655

sight of him, he beckoned with his hand. Roe had a clock with him, and this he presented. Clocks at that time were not manufactured in the East. Ricci, the Jesuit, made a good impression with one in 1600 at the Court of China. They represented that first application of Western science and mathematics to practical mechanics which afterwards was to give Europe such overwhelming power. But, of course, Jahangir had no inkling that from the little mechanism ticking under his hand would grow engines which one day would strike down all Asia. He was pleased and said bluntly, " What do you want of me ? " " Justice," replied Roe, and he detailed certain pressing injustices under which the English traders lived at Surat, particularly how they were robbed and insulted by the local officials. Jahangir immediately issued orders for the remedying of these abuses. In the months that followed Roe patiently pursued a negotiation that became drawn out into years and was not concluded until September, 1618, three years after he had landed in India. When he understood what he calls the " pace of the Court," that is, the strength of the various parties, and was sure that he could always obtain a hearing from the Emperor, who had got to like him, he cleverly decided not to force the pro-Portuguese faction into open hostility by persuading Jahangir to pass orders over its head, but to try and win it over by fair argument, while letting it be known that if he were refused justice against all reason he would appeal to the Emperor. Asaf Khan, the Empress's brother, was the person with whom he dealt directly. This lord was very rude at first, but Roe never abated an inch of dignity, and when on one occasion he was summoned by Asaf Khan and kept waiting deliberately, he sent him in this tart message : " If your greatness were no more than your manners you would not dare to use me so." It paid to stand up to the Mughals.

The final settlement was not exactly the treaty between Jahangir and King James which he had come to get, but it was a satisfying compromise. He obtained a public declaration by the Emperor of his amity towards the East India Company at Surat. The merchants were given liberty to trade freely, to live in a rented house on shore, to govern themselves and to bear arms when they went abroad in the city. No payments beyond the normal dues were to be demanded of them. The Portuguese were invited to co-operate in an open trade.

A settlement is best judged by its actual results. This one had the effect of giving the East India Company enough security to carry on its trade with profit, an advantage that sufficed to lay the foundations of the power which eventually enabled the British to supplant the Mughal as lords of India.

THE ENGLISH QUARTERS AT SURAT
An eighteenth century engraving

## CHAPTER THREE

## SAMUEL WHITE : MERCHANT-INTERLOPER
### (1650—1689)

AS we have seen, the East India Company was a monopoly. To be more precise, it was a royal monopoly, deriving from the King's prerogative and not from statute law. By the time of Charles II public opinion had turned more and more against royal monopolies. Indeed, by then it had been held by the judicature that the King had no power to grant them inside the realm. In 1683 a test case was brought to determine whether he could grant them outside the realm, with special reference to the East India Company's monopoly in Asia. It came before the notorious Judge Jeffreys and he found for the Crown.

This verdict was very pleasing to the Company's shareholders, a small clique of about forty persons closely connected with the Court. A few years previously their stock was valued at £1,700,000, on which the dividends averaged 22 per cent. Jeffrey's verdict guaranteed their future profits. But it is one thing to lay down the law and another to enforce it. To prevent Englishmen who were not shareholders in the Company from trading in Asia was impossible. From the beginning there had always been men who refused to recognise the Company's monopoly and sailed East in their own ships. Claiming that they typified the spirit of independence which was England's glory, they called themselves Free Merchants, though by the members of the Company they were dubbed Interlopers. The most remarkable of these Interlopers was Samuel White.

Samuel White started life as an employee of the Company, sailing East in 1675 on board one of their ships, the *Loyal Subject*, in the capacity of mate. Sixty years had passed since Roe had set the Company on its feet at Surat. During these years it had drawn level with and then passed the Portuguese as far as India was concerned. The Dutch, by taking Malacca, had also got the better of them and proceeded to lay the foundations of what is now the Dutch Empire of Java, Sumatra and the adjacent islands. After the Dutch came the French, who established a small trade with India and were interesting themselves in the possibilities of Siam. These events almost eliminated the Portuguese and resulted in the trade to and from Asia being mostly handled by the English and the Dutch. Surat remained the headquarters of the East India Company, which had acquired subsidiary trading settlements at Bombay, Madras, Hugli and certain intermediate ports. Its policy was unchanged. "Our business is only trade and security, not conquest," wrote Sir Josiah Child, President of the Court of Directors at this period. Conquest, indeed, was out of the question, because the Mughal Empire, though it had passed its zenith, was still very strong. The trade consisted in the buying of cotton goods in India, for cash or in exchange for English manufactures. But there was another trade, known as the country trade, the exchange of commodities between the various countries inside Asia. The Company was not interested in that trade, which was carried on by the local inhabitants and the Interlopers. But the employees of the Company were allowed to engage in it for their private profit in a half open partnership with the Interlopers. Thus, there existed a good deal of give and take between the East India Company and the Free Merchants. As long as the latter confined themselves to the country trade and made no attempt to compete in the London cotton market or embarrass the regular trade by agreements with native rulers contrary to its interests, their activities, though not officially recognised, were winked at.

This was the world, these were the possibilities, to which Samuel White had arrived when the *Loyal Subject* landed him at Madras in 1676. As an

AN INCIDENT IN THE WARS BETWEEN THE SIAMESE AND BURMESE

A 17th or 18th century painting by a Siamese artist

A MALAYAN VILLAGE

Coloured aquatint from T. and W. Daniell's *Picturesque Voyage to India by the Way of China*, 1810

employee of the Company he had a ridiculously small salary, £10 a year, with the prospect later on of promotion and private trade. If he did not die of fever or dysentery he might hope to return to England in ten or fifteen years with a modest fortune. But White was not a person for whom the modest, the safe and the slow had any appeal. He wanted a large fortune in a hurry and he was prepared to run desperate risks to obtain it. The interloping trade gave a man of his character, vehement, enterprising and without scruples, exactly the opportunity which he required. And an opening happened to be ready for him, for his brother, George, was established as a Free Merchant at Ayudhya, the capital of Siam.

At that time Ayudhya was an important centre of the country trade, for it was the emporium where Chinese and Japanese goods were exchanged for Indian goods. The trade route was from Canton by sea to Ayudhya; thence overland to Mergui, a port on the eastern shores of the Bay of Bengal and in Siamese territory; and so across the Bay to Masulipatam, some two hundred miles north of Madras. Samuel White took an early opportunity of visiting his brother, travelling to Mergui and thence to Ayudhya.

The East India Company had agents in Ayudhya, as had the Dutch and French companies. There were also many Free Merchants. The King of Siam, Phra Narai, was a man of vision. Unlike the Great Mughal and the Son of Heaven, he seems to have grasped the significance of the European irruption into Asia and to have argued that if he could westernise his army and increase his wealth by trade with Europe he would make Siam the most powerful kingdom in the Indo-Chinese peninsula, able not only to resist her Asiatic rivals, but to face the danger of European, particularly Dutch, encroachments. To achieve this he must get the assistance of a European state. He did not trust the Dutch and this left him the choice between the English and the French.

When Samuel White reached Ayudhya the King was beginning to enlist Englishmen in his service, and George White had no difficulty in procuring for his brother an appointment as Captain of one of the King's ships plying between Mergui and Masulipatam. This was in 1677, and for six years Samuel White sailed backwards and forwards across the Bay of Bengal, delivering the royal cargo—it was elephants—and trading on his own account. Meanwhile a friend of his brother George's, a Greek adventurer called Constant Phaulkon, had attracted the King's attention. He was a man of enormous talent and ambition. To the King he seemed the very person to carry out the new policy. He was appointed Minister and soon became the most powerful figure in the kingdom. On his advice the King decided to look to France rather than to England for the arms and military assistance he required. Time would elapse before these could materialise and it was decided to take certain preliminary steps with the help of the English Interlopers in the Siamese service.

Accordingly, White was sent for in 1683, created Mandarin and made Shabandar of Mergui, an appointment which combined the duties of a Superintendent of Trade and a Commissioner of Maritime Affairs. He was instructed to fortify Mergui and get together a fleet of armed merchantmen so that when the French arrived Mergui would already be a port of the first importance on the Canton–Masulipatam trade route, a base where the French ships could anchor and from which with their assistance Siam could dominate the Bay of Bengal. The plan was a direct threat to the East India Company, whose ships commanded the Bay and its approaches.

In accepting this appointment White placed himself in a situation which was bound sooner or later to bring him into conflict with the East India Company. But his eyes were fixed entirely on the fortune which his new appointment would enable him to make as an interloper. He did not care whether he hurt the Company or not, nor had he the slightest intention of working as the faithful servant of the King of Siam. Mergui was a week's journey by forest track and river from Ayudhya and he calculated that supervision would be lax and that he would be free to pursue his private ends without interference.

As soon as some of the armed ships which he was authorised to build or purchase were available, he placed them under the command of English interloper captains and, declaring an unprovoked war on Burma and Golconda, an Indian kingdom independent of the Mughal, without the knowledge or sanction of the Siamese Government, proceeded to seize all ships belonging to those states which were encountered in the Bay of Bengal. Then, manning the prizes with his own crews, he sent them to ports in Sumatra or the Persian Gulf, where their cargoes were sold as his private property. For two years he continued to prey on native shipping in this manner without being called to account by the Siamese Government. His profits enabled him to remit home £15,740 and to keep by him a trading capital in cash and jewels of a like amount, a total which nowadays would be equivalent to at least £150,000. Besides this commerce with other people's property, he made very free with the money granted to him by the Siamese treasury, for he embezzled the entire sum allotted for the fortification of Mergui and, by maintaining a garrison which only existed on paper, was able on pay-day to credit himself with their wages.

Public opinion in the Siam of the date was not very vocal, but such was the indignation in Mergui at his contemptuous disregard of his duty that

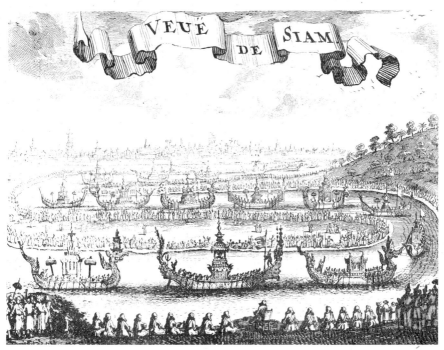

VIEW OF SIAM
Engraving from le père Guy Tachard's *Voyage de Siam des Pères Jésuites*, 1688

complaint was made to the Government and he was recalled to Ayudhya in 1686 to explain the charges against him. He survived the enquiry through a combination of circumstances. Phaulkon stood by him, partly because he seems to have had some share in White's profits and also because George White, now in England, was acting for him there. Moreover, he knew that, brilliant though his position was, it was also precarious, because the Mandarinate disliked his policy, believing that if the French secured a hold on the country it would lose its independence. White, he thought, could be trusted to support him against a possible rebellion. He therefore quashed the enquiry proceedings and sent him back to Mergui with increased powers. This convinced White that he had little more time in which to enrich himself. In a heart to heart talk with Francis Davenport, his secretary, he said one day: "To tell you truly, I am not without strong apprehensions that his Lordship stands but in a slippery place and in case he once slips how can I expect to keep my footing. I am resolved to make Hay while the Sun shines and so be in readiness for any Revolution that may happen."

On arrival at Mergui he moored below his house a new frigate he had built called the *Resolution*, and began loading it with money, jewels and a rich cargo, so that he could escape to England at a moment's notice. But another, and a more formidable, danger was looming on the horizon. The East India Company had come to the conclusion that he must be suppressed. As a private individual he had obliged them by putting trade in their way, but his depredations in the Bay had upset their official commerce. Moreover, he was now associated with Phaulkon's French policy. If the French established themselves at Mergui, immediately opposite Madras and on the route to the Far East, the whole position of the Company was potentially threatened. They therefore procured from James II, who was a large shareholder, an order recalling White from service with the Crown of Siam and sent a frigate called the *Curtana* to Mergui, commanded by a Captain Weltden, whose orders were to bring White to Madras, there to stand his trial.

The *Curtana* arrived at the bar of Mergui on 23 June, 1687. Then began a strange drama. White knew that to go to Madras with Weltden meant ruin and possibly death on a charge of piracy or treason. To fight Weltden would also be a capital offence, for which, if he escaped afterwards to England, he could be arrested and tried. To flee to Ayudhya was equally desperate, as Phaulkon's régime was now tottering : he would be murdered there. The dilemma was appalling, but he saw a way out.

Weltden was very poor and he began by offering him a chance to make money. Getting friendly with him in this way he persuaded him that the charges of piracy and treason were malicious and that he was a much wronged, worthy gentleman. He also professed perfect willingness to go to Madras.

Meanwhile he had told the Siamese Council at Mergui that Weltden had come to seize their town and secretly encouraged them to resist. It was arranged that they should send fire-boats down on the tide and burn the *Curtana*. So friendly, however, did White appear to become with Weltden that the Siamese thought he was tricking them and must have bought his own immunity by promising to deliver Mergui to the English. They therefore decided, in addition to burning the *Curtana*, to kill him and the numerous interloping Englishmen who had settled in Mergui. The attack took place on the night of 14 July, 1687. White narrowly escaped death by taking refuge in the *Resolution*. His house was burnt and some eighty Englishmen were killed. But the fire-boats failed to set the *Curtana* alight and both ships cleared the port in safety.

White then persuaded Weltden that the Siamese attempt to murder him was proof of his loyalty to King James. Weltden, quite convinced of his innocence, believed him when he said he would accompany him to Madras and became so lax that White was able to give him the slip one day and sail for England with all his treasure.

He got there long before any news of his recent doings at Mergui had reached the Company's Directors. Moreover, James II had just fled the realm and William and the Whigs had come in. The Whigs had always been opposed to royal monopolies. White saw his chance: he would anticipate any charges which the Company might subsequently bring by himself sueing them for damages to the extent of £40,000. But he died suddenly in May, 1689, before the case came on. Phaulkon had lost his life the previous year in the expected revolution.

Mary and Susan, White's daughters, succeeded to the fortune.

## CHAPTER FOUR

## ROBERT CLIVE : MERCHANT-SOLDIER
### (1725–1774)

THE next date is 1744, for it was on 1 June of that year and at seven in the evening that Robert Clive landed at Madras to take up his appointment as clerk to the East India Company on a salary of five pounds per annum. He was aged nineteen, of neurotic temperament and subject to fits.

During the sixty-six years which had elapsed since White defied the East India Company, it had undergone a change in constitution but not in policy. The agitation against it, of which White's petition to Parliament was a part, culminated in a resolution of the Commons in 1694 that " all subjects of England have equal rights to trade in the East Indies, unless prohibited by Act of Parliament." The trade being thus thrown open, the Interlopers founded a rival Company. It was discovered, however, that this was not good business. Neither Company prospered. Accordingly, in 1708 the new Company became fused with the old, with the result that, since the combined shareholders were now fairly representative of all interests, the united Company was no longer a harmful monopoly. As to its policy, that remained trade and security, not conquest. Though its trading ports at Bombay, Madras and Calcutta were fortified to resist attack from the sea by European, and from the land by Asiatic, adventurers, they were in all other respects no more than emporiums for the exchange of English manufactures and Indian cotton goods. They served, moreover, as settlements on the way to China, where the Company also had its factory and agents. The story of its progress at Canton cannot be told here. Suffice it to say that by the middle of the eighteenth century England had in peace-time a secured trade route via the Cape eastwards to the opposite side of the globe. The wealth, knowledge and opportunities which this afforded led during the century to the discovery of Australia, New Zealand and Oceania and eventually to that migration overseas of the British people which produced the phenomenon of the new British Empire—the old British Empire having come to an end with the loss of the American colonies. The first step towards the founding of that Empire was the change of policy from peaceful trading to territorial expansion which force of circumstances obliged the East India Company to make at the very time when Clive landed in India. He was fated to put the new policy into execution, and his success was so much greater than was expected that the conquest of all India followed inevitably. Clive's arrival was concurrent with an event of the first importance. The

ROBERT CLIVE
Engraving by F. Bartolozzi after N. Dance

Mughal Empire, which to Roe had seemed so imposing, was breaking up. The officials who governed its provinces were turning into independent princes and were making war upon one another. The imperial administration, essential to trade, was ceasing to function. In what manner could the Company steer a peaceful way through such dangerous perplexities? Before it had decided how to protect itself and its dividends from the threatened anarchy, the Company of French merchants trading to India showed the way. At the head of them was a man very different from the cautious English merchants. He was an adventurer and, instead of merely strengthening the fortifications of the French emporium at Pondicherry and hoping for the best, he resolved to take sides in the scramble for kingdoms which was beginning in that part of India and, by backing a successful claimant, obtain from him concessions which would make the French, not the English, the leading merchants in India. This forced the East India Company to abandon its old policy. If it were to survive it must fight the French and their partisans, and it must support rival partisans.

It continued to believe that the fight was only for trade and security, but actually it was for the mastery of India.

Two years after his arrival Clive was transferred from the commercial to the military side. He had been a queer and homesick clerk, but now found he possessed a natural aptitude for soldiering. In 1747 he was made ensign, in 1749 lieutenant, and by 1752, aged twenty-seven, had become captain. He was noted for coolness in action and for that feeling for the rhythm of a battle which has always been the mark of the born military leader. It was largely thanks to the military genius of this young man that the Company got the better of the French and by 1753 secured for the throne of the Carnatic, the area of the coast where Madras and Pondicherry were situated, a prince favourable to English interests.

The Directors would gladly then have returned to their former trading and sent Clive back to his desk but, having once become entangled in Indian politics, they found it impossible to extricate themselves. In 1756, Suraj-ud-Dowlah, who had the position of Nawab or Viceroy of Bengal, though actually he was independent of the Empire, descended upon the Company's settlement at Calcutta, defeated the garrison, burnt the town, and shut up one stifling night of June a hundred and forty-four of his English prisoners in a barrack cell, 18 by 14 feet, where most of them suffocated. It seems he was instigated to attack by the French, whose settlement at Chandernagore was near Calcutta. The catastrophe roused the merchants of Madras, and after long confabulations they decided to send an expedition to retake Calcutta.

Clive, who had just returned from a year's leave in England, was appointed to command it. He was only thirty-one years of age, but his services in the Carnatic campaigns had been so distinguished—his defence of Arcot had made him a hero—that the Directors in London had procured him a colonelcy and given him a seat on the Madras Council. The expeditionary force was composed of six hundred white troops and one thousand sepoys. Clive felt that he had been entrusted with a task of great moment. Though the other members of the Council had no idea that to restore the situation in Bengal would mean more than a return to the safe trading they had previously enjoyed there, he had an intuition that he was about to make history. " This expedition, if attended with success, may enable me to do great things," he wrote to his father ; and to the London Committee he declared : " I flatter myself that this Expedition will not end with the retaking of Calcutta only."

It certainly did not end with the retaking of Calcutta. That was a small matter, for the Nawab, having reduced it to ruins and not expecting an English counter-attack, had left few troops in the neighbourhood. But when he heard that Clive had re-occupied it, he marched against him with an immense force.

32

A VIEW OF THE NEW GOVERNMENT HOUSE, CALCUTTA, BUILT IN 1802

Coloured aquatint by J. Clarke and H. Merke after Moffat, c.1807

A VIEW OF KUTRA MOSQUE BUILT BY MIR JAFFIER AT MURSHIDABAD

Coloured aquatint from William Hodge's *Select Views in India*, 1786

Clive would have had no chance at all if Suraj-ud-Dowlah had been a viceroy of the Mughal Empire in its prime. But the prince represented no one but himself, and his government and generals were corrupt and cowardly. Painfully aware that he might be displaced by a rival at any time, he had no confidence in his troops. When the Indians reached the gardens near the town, Clive penetrated their lines in a thick mist at dawn and alarmed them so much that the Nawab opened negotiations, offering to recognize the English return to Calcutta.

But Clive saw that this would be no permanent settlement. The Nawab and the French of Chandernagore were in league and, if the expedition were withdrawn, the Nawab could not be trusted. To make Calcutta safe two measures were necessary, the destruction of the French and the replacement of Suraj-ud-Dowlah by another prince ready to further British trade, as had been done in the Carnatic. Accordingly he attacked Chandernagore and took it, thereafter entering into a correspondence with Mir Jaffier, the Nawab's uncle, who was offered the throne for his help. Mir Jaffier had not the smallest respect for his nephew and declared that if Clive marched on the Nawab's capital of Murshidabad he would join him with the forces under his command.

Murshidabad was some hundred and fifty miles north of Calcutta. To attack it with 613 European foot, 91 half-castes, 10 guns and 2,100 sepoys— for such were the exact forces at Clive's disposal at the moment—was a wild imprudence. The Nawab's army consisted of 15,000 cavalry, 35,000 infantry and 53 heavy guns, mostly served by French gunners. Mir Jaffier had promised to come over, but had given not the smallest guarantee of good faith. Defeat meant not only the annihilation of the expedition but a second sack of Calcutta, perhaps a second Black Hole. But Clive marched.

At a place called Katwa, seventy miles up the road, he expected to find Mir Jaffier and his men. The prince, however, failed to keep the appointment and Clive had to decide whether to cross the Hugli, which at that point lay across his path, and with that large river in his rear, which the approaching monsoon would cause to flood, press on against an army sixteen times the size of his own and sitting comfortably in front of its entrenched base. Against the advice of his officers and the whole experience of war he decided to cross.

At Plassey, a large mango grove twenty miles further on, he suddenly was confronted with the Nawab's host. The battle which ensued has been the subject of much writing since that June day a hundred and eighty-four years ago, but no one has succeeded in fully explaining how Clive won it. Perhaps the chief reason was that it did not occur to the men of the old Thirty-ninth, the modern Dorsets, who formed the bulk of Clive's white troops, that they could be beaten.

When the battle was won and Mir Jaffier saw it was safe to cross over, he joined Clive, and together they took Murshidabad. He was installed as Nawab and in the vast area of Bengal, the gateway to upper India, the British found they could do what they liked. The Directors still cherished the hope of returning to plain business, but the native administration went to pieces and eventually they were obliged to substitute their own, which in the course of a century was gradually extended over the rest of India.

After the prodigious stroke of Plassey, which is one of the decisive battles of the world though only twenty-three men were killed on the British side, the rest of Clive's life was a series of misfortunes. He had gone out to India as a merchant with the object of making money and now turned his attention again to this matter. Mir Jaffier paid him £160,000 down for his help, and he acquired jewels worth a million pounds in modern values. Moreover, he secured a great estate in Bengal so that on his return to England his income amounted to £40,000 per annum, a fortune which he declared was no more than a " genteel competence," for it might have been much larger if he had taken full advantage of his opportunities.

Had he retired into private life with his money all would have been well enough. But, having been created a peer, he sought to make himself felt in the Government. He was no politician, however, and in 1764, seven years after Plassey, accepted the Presidentship of the Council of Calcutta. There he tried to prevent the employees of the Company from enriching themselves by corrupt practices which the weak native Government was unable to stop. He failed because his colleagues declared that he with his large fortune had no right to restrain them. This caused a return of his neurosis and he became again subject to fits. " It grieved me beyond measure," wrote at this time his friend Carnac, " to see a Person endued with such extraordinary firmness oppressed in his spirits as to exceed any degree of hysterics I was ever witness to." In this state he returned to England in 1767.

There his enemies engineered an attack on him, nominally on moral grounds but really from malice. He was charged with having abused his position after Plassey by acquiring enormous wealth. For two years he was subjected to an inquisition by a Select Committee of the Commons, and though in the end he was allowed to keep his fortune, and his great services were acknowledged, the strain had been too much for his nervous temperament and he committed suicide at the age of forty-nine.

To-day his statue stands on the steps of the India Office looking down upon St. James's Park. Though no adequate biography of him exists, he is one of the best known of England's worthies, largely because Macaulay wrote an essay about him which is read in all schools.

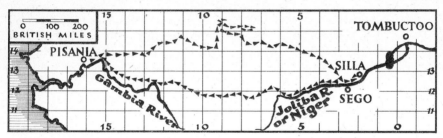

DIAGRAM OF MUNGO PARK'S JOURNEY OF EXPLORATION TO DISCOVER THE RIVER NIGER
Drawn from the map compiled by J. Rennell from Mungo Park's notes

CHAPTER FIVE

## MUNGO PARK : MERCHANT-EXPLORER
### (1771–1806)

THE four previous sketches have suggested how Asia was opened to international commerce. The case of Africa was very different. In the late 18th century nothing was known at first hand of any part of the tropical interior of that continent. There were rumours of a river called the Niger and that it crossed Africa near the 15th parallel, but no white man had ever seen it. Some believed it to be the Senegal or the Gambia ; others argued that it was a tributary of the Nile or of the Congo ; others again declared it to be the Congo itself, for no large river had been observed to fall into the sea between the mouth of the Gambia and of the Congo. Timbuktu lay somewhere on its banks, a fabulously rich city, roofed, it was declared, with solid gold.

The Mediterranean coast of Africa had, of course, always been known and the other immense coasts to the Cape and up to the southern end of the Red Sea had been explored by the Portuguese in the 16th century on their way to India. Later, when the plantations in the West Indies and in America developed, it was learned that the Moslem inhabitants of Africa were prepared to sell negro slaves to Europeans. From the time of Elizabeth onwards the English engaged in this slave trade. Through agents stationed principally near the mouth of the Gambia they established touch with the Moslem slavers, who marched down their living merchandise from the interior to the ships waiting to carry it across the Atlantic. This export, together with a little ivory and gum, was the extent of the African trade for two centuries.

35

Towards the end of the 18th century, however, men began to argue that the great African continent must yield many other profitable commodities. For instance, it had long been said to be rich in gold. But these were rumours which only exploration could verify. Timbuktu, the alleged centre of the continental trade, must be reached. If it lay on the Niger, then the course of that river must be traced.

With these objects in view, the African Association was founded in 1788, a year after Wilberforce had begun his crusade against slavery. The first man to be sent out by this body was a Major Houghton, but he died in 1791 before reaching the Niger. His place was taken by Mungo Park, the subject of this chapter.

Park was born in 1771, the son of a small Scottish farmer of the vale of Yarrow. A quiet, studious and earnest youth, he worked his way up to a degree in medicine at Edinburgh University and sailed to Sumatra as surgeon on an East India Company's ship. On his return he was introduced to Sir Joseph Banks, the founder of the African Association, and shortly afterwards agreed to go and search for the Niger. At that time he was only twenty-four years of age.

At the beginning of the diary which he kept of his travels, he gives both the objects of his journey and a glimpse of his own modest and resolute character. " If I should perish in my journey, I was willing that my hopes and expectations should perish with me ; and if I should succeed in rendering the geography of Africa more familiar to my countrymen, and in opening to their ambition and industry new sources of wealth and new channels of commerce, I knew that I was in the hands of men of honour, who would not fail to bestow that remuneration which my successful services would appear to them to merit."

In June, 1795, he reached the Gambia and lodged in the house of a Mr. Laidley, a slaver who lived at Pisania, some distance up the river. The village was no more than a clearing in the vast forest beside the steaming tidal water, and there he waited till the rains were over, learning Mandingo, the most useful negro language.

In December he set out for the unknown interior, riding a horse, wearing a blue coat and a top-hat, and accompanied by two negro servants. His course was eastwards, through the dominions of independent negro kings, amiable, greedy, ridiculous ruffians. The first of them was Almani of Fatteconda, on whom he called to pay his respects on December 21. This potentate was fascinated by his blue coat and umbrella and obliged him to offer them both as a present. As Park penetrated further, this kind of robbery became more ruinous, until King Tiggity Sego took three quarters of what remained to him

MUNGO PARK
Engraving from Mungo Park's *Travels*, 1816

on the plea of customs duty. Rapacious though they were, however, these pagan monarchs plundered him without malice and he was perfectly safe in their dominions.

But further east there lived less manageable rulers, the Moslem sultans who preyed on the Pagans. After crossing the upper waters of the Senegal he entered their territories. These Sultanates had been founded centuries before by Arabs from the Mediterranean littoral, who by intermarriage with the indigenous negroes had become a race of halfcastes, rather similar in appearance, says Park, to the mulattoes of the West Indies. In character they were like the worst type of Arab, malicious, cruel and ferociously bigoted. Park's method of securing the goodwill of kings on his route was always to make them presents, but on entering the domains of Sultan Ali of Benaun in March, 1796, he was arrested by minions of that prince before he had had time to take this precaution. " Ali was sitting upon a black leather cushion, clipping a few hairs from his upper lip, a female attendant holding up a looking-glass before

A VIEW OF ALI'S TENT AT THE CAMP OF BENAUN
Engraving from Mungo Park's *Travels*, 1816

him," records Park. " He appeared to be an old man, of the Arab cast, with a long white beard : and he had sullen and indignant aspect." Park was abominably treated by him and his people, being detained a prisoner, robbed of all he possessed, subjected to every indignity which malice could devise, and given only one small meal a day. As an example of his miseries, one scorching night in May, having been harshly refused water, he crept out to the cattle troughs where " kneeling down, I thrust my head between two of the cows, and drank with great pleasure, until the water was nearly exhausted, and the cows began to contend with each other for the last mouthful." In these trials Park exhibited an extraordinary patience and mildness, neither resisting his cruel treatment nor repining, being seemingly upheld by some inner certainty that he would reach the mysterious river of his dreams.

Not till the end of June did he escape from this grievous servitude, being aided in some measure by Ali's wife, Fatima, who had been won by his handsome face. Prim to a degree though he was, Park moved the hearts of many women in Africa.

Thanks to Fatima he was able to escape with his horse, his servants and his clothes, which now consisted of two shirts, two pairs of trousers, two

A VIEW OF A BRIDGE OVER THE BA-FING OR RIVER NIGER
Engraving from Mungo Park's *Travels,* 1816

handkerchiefs, two waistcoats, his riding boots, cloak and top-hat, in the lining of which were concealed his notes. He had no valuables of any kind with which to pay his way, but undaunted, indeed dauntless, he headed on for the Niger, now reported to lie some 250 miles to the South East. Here the land was desert and very soon he was suffering terribly from thirst. His horse could carry him no further, his servants had deserted him and he fell to the ground exhausted, expecting death. " I cast," he writes in his stilted way, " a last look on the surrounding scene, and whilst I reflected on the awful change that was about to take place, this world with its enjoyment seemed to vanish from my recollection." A sudden thunderstorm saved his life. Revived, he pressed on, and at last on 21st July, "looking forwards, I saw with infinite pleasure the great object of my mission—the long-sought-for majestic Niger, glittering to the morning sun, as broad as the Thames at Westminster, and flowing slowly *to the eastward.* I hastened to the brink, and having drunk of the water, lifted up my fervent thanks in prayer to the Great Ruler of all things, for having thus far crowned my endeavours with success."

That the Niger flowed East and not West cleared up one point which had been long in doubt. But where did it flow to? Did it turn South to the sea or go on across Africa to join the Congo or the Nile? With unquenchable spirit Park went on alone to find the answer to these questions. Actually he was about 1,800 miles from the Niger mouth, which is concealed in a delta of mangrove swamps in the Gulf of Guinea.

After walking about a hundred miles along the North bank he saw that it was hopeless to proceed, for he was entering again a Moslem Sultanate, where imprisonment and slavery inevitably awaited him. " Worn down by sickness, exhausted with hunger and fatigue, half naked, and without any article of value by which I might procure provisions, clothes or lodging . . . I was now convinced that the obstacle to my further progress was insurmountable." He turned back with a heavy heart, for he learnt that he was only twelve days' march from Timbuktu.

The hardships on his journey back to the coast were much greater than on the way out. On 25th August he met a band of robbers. He still possessed his horse, his top-hat, and the clothes he stood up in. The robbers only left him a shirt and trousers, " but, as they went away, one of them threw back my hat, in the crown of which I kept my memorandums, and this was probably the reason why they did not wish to keep it," he writes, meaning that they thought the writing was magic and unsafe to tamper with.

Lying helpless and alone in the tropical forest, five hundred miles from the nearest European settlement, Park was nearer giving up hope than on any previous occasion. " But at this moment," he records in a characteristic passage, "the extraordinary beauty of a small moss in fructification irresistibly caught my eye . . . Can the Being, thought I, who planted, watered and brought to perfection, in this obscure part of the world, a thing which appears of so small importance, look with unconcern upon the situation and sufferings of creatures formed after His own image ? " This reflection comforted him and certain that all would be well, he got on to his feet and trudged on. He was not disappointed, for the negroes at the next village treated him with kindness.

His diary now becomes of particular interest. He joined a gang of slaves, who were being marched down to the coast, and his account of what he saw is strangely moving. At no part of his narrative, however, does it occur to him to denounce slavery as an institution. He is sorry for the slaves, but accepts their state as part of the nature of things. Though a man of the highest character, mild-mannered and pious, the humanitarianism of his great contemporary, Wilberforce, would have seemed to him over enthusiastic.

On 11th June, 1797, he reached Pisania and Mr. Laidley, who had long given him up for dead, and in October was safely home in England. In 1805 the African Association sent him out again, this time in command of a well-equipped party. But three-quarters of his companions were dead of fever and exhaustion

MODE OF TRAVELLING IN AFRICA

Coloured aquatint by I. Clark after W. Hutton. From W. Hutton's *Voyage to Africa*, 1821

A JAVAN IN COURT DRESS

Coloured aquatint from Raffles's *History of Java*, 1807

before he reached the Niger, this time by another route. There the remnant embarked in a canoe and followed the river past Timbuktu and for a thousand miles, until, while still some 800 miles from its mouth, they were all killed by tribesmen at the rapids of Boussa. Not until thirty-three years later was the mouth located.

As the 19th century passed, the whole interior of Africa was mapped and partitioned. The slave-trade was abolished, the Gambia region becoming for that reason impoverished; the Negro kings and Moslem Sultans lost their independence; new sources of wealth and channels for commerce, openings for European ambition and industry, were, as Park had hoped, developed. Central Africa for the first time in its long dark history was brought into contact with the centres of civilization and entered upon a course, the end of which is not in sight.

CHAPTER SIX

# THOMAS STAMFORD RAFFLES : MERCHANT-ADMINISTRATOR
## (1781–1829)

HAD the scheme of this book permitted, the adventures of the British in America might have been illustrated by some typical career. That not being possible, it should be noted at least that when on 19th October, 1781, Cornwallis surrendered to Washington at York Town, the British dominion in America came to an end. England was thus thrown back upon the territories and trading points she had acquired in Asia. These, as we have seen, pivoted upon India and reached on to China through the Malayan straits which the Dutch had made the centre of their trade operations.

Suddenly Napoleon strode upon the scene. He annexed Holland outright in 1810, and so acquired the Cape of Good Hope, Ceylon and the great islands of Sumatra, Java and Borneo. India was thus encircled and it was his grand plan to drive the British out of that continent by an advance based on the Dutch possessions. To spike that plan it was decided in June, 1811, to seize Java, the strategic centre of his whole operation. The Governor-General of India was then Lord Minto, and he led the expedition in person. His secretary was Stamford Raffles, a young man of thirty.

Raffles was born off Jamaica on 6 July, 1781, on board a merchant ship of which his father was Master. He was brought up in London, and at the early age of fourteen a clerkship was secured for him at the East India House, the London headquarters of the East India Company, as his family was too poor to support him longer. In this humble appointment he displayed much assiduity and continued his education out of office hours. In 1800 he was promoted to a post worth £100 a year and, continuing to impress his superiors by his extraordinary industry, was appointed in 1805 Assistant Secretary on a salary of £1,500 a year to the Governor of Penang, a trading port on an island off the Malay Peninsula, which the Company had recently acquired by arrangement with the local Sultan. Here again he became remarkable for his unceasing toil and the exceptional interest which he took in everything which concerned the country. By 1810, though only twenty-nine years of age, he was considered the greatest authority on that part of the world. In manner he was amiable and high-spirited, and his character was essentially humane and lovable. These qualities and qualifications attracted the attention of Lord Minto, and thus it was that he became the Governor-General's personal assistant in the expedition to Java, an appointment which carried him into the great world-stream of the Napoleonic war.

The British taking of Java in 1811 from the Dutch and French was an analogous operation to the taking in 1941 of Syria from the French and Germans. It was effected in three months without much difficulty, the British casualties being 633, and the Franco-Dutch 7,000. Raffles was then appointed Lieutenant-Governor of Java.

His administration of the island was very remarkable. He was, it should be remembered, in the employ of the merchants of the East India Company, whose first preoccupation was to secure dividends. It is true that in India, after Clive had opened the way to political dominion and Warren Hastings had organized a civil service which reflected British ideals of law and justice, the Company had advanced a distance beyond the strictly commercial point of view that had been its strength in early days. Responsibility for the native inhabitants was there admitted. But outside India, in Penang, for instance,

SIR THOMAS STAMFORD RAFFLES
Engraving from D. C. Boulger's *Life of Sir Stamford Raffles*, 1897

the only duty of the Company's officials was to foster trade. It was therefore quite remarkable that Raffles in his administration of Java should have set himself with indefatigable zeal to improve the condition of the islanders. Indeed, he was the first outside India to put in practice the new principle of trusteeship for backward races, then hardly accepted or understood beyond the small body of reformers and humanitarians of whom Wilberforce was the principal. In this respect he differs from Park, who, though humane by temperament, saw no compelling reason why the oppression of the weak was unworthy of the England for whose glory he died. In 1814, writing of the work of the officials he had appointed, Raffles says : " Placed in situations which, but a few years ago, were considered only as affording a fortune to the individual . . . they have without exception felt the honour and character of the British nation prompt them above every selfish consideration and in six months enabled me to effect a revolution which two centuries of Dutch administration could scarcely dream of." In a memorandum dated 1810 he had written that the Dutch policy in Java was "a more cold-blooded, illiberal and ungenerous policy

43

than has ever been exhibited towards any country, unless we except the conduct of the European nations towards the slave-coast of Africa." But Raffles' principles cost money, and as the Directors were business men and not humanitarian reformers, they were by no means enthusiastic about him and his idea that the primary object of his government should be the welfare of the Javanese.

The fall of Napoleon put an end to Raffles' work in Java, for Holland, as one of the main pegs in the European balance, had to be restored to her original position, and in consequence all her overseas possessions except the Cape and Ceylon were returned to her. This was a great blow to Raffles, who on the termination of his appointment took leave and returned to England. Though coldly received by the magnates of the East India House, he was welcomed by the scientific world as an oriental savant, for during his eleven years in Asia his intellectual curiosity had driven him to make extensive studies in the botany, zoology, art and history of Malaya and Java. He had brought back with him, moreover, part of his collections, and his contributions to knowledge were received with such acclaim that society lionized him until finally the Prince Regent bade him to a levee and, " expressing the high sense he entertained of the eminent services he had rendered to his country in the government of Java," made him a knight. This obliged the India House to look on him with more favour, and in 1817 he was appointed Lieutenant-Governor of Bencoolen, a small possession of the Company's on the west coast of Sumatra.

The situation in Sumatra was this. The Dutch held the south end of the great island. The rest of the thousand miles of its length was ruled by small Sultans. Bencoolen was a mere trading post. Raffles and his newly married wife, fresh from the excitements and delights of the London season, found themselves in a deadly little hole, " the roads impassable, the highways of the town overrun with rank grass, the Government house a den of ravenous dogs and polecats." However, this was the sort of thing that stimulated Raffles. He conceived almost at once the idea of making Bencoolen the capital of Sumatra, of inducing the Sultans to accept him as overlord and of developing the country for the benefit of its inhabitants. So extraordinary and indefatigable a man was he, that he might well have accomplished this feat, had not the Dutch become alarmed, for they knew Raffles well and did not doubt that his personality would suffice to bring the Sultans under English influence. This would have meant for all practical purposes the loss of Sumatra, though under the peace settlement the whole island had been declared their sphere. Accordingly they took steps to extend their effective occupation and to put every difficulty they could in the way of British commerce throughout the whole region of the Islands. This policy ran counter to the trade agreements

A RONG'GENG OR DANCING GIRL
Aquatint from Raffles's *History of Java*, 1817

embodied in the peace settlement and profoundly disturbed the Directors at home. They blamed Raffles' forward policy and complained to Canning, who on his side had been assailed by protests from the Dutch Government. Canning and his colleagues were more concerned with maintaining the stability of Europe and the friendliest relations with the new kingdom of the Netherlands than with the expansion of British trade in rivalry with the Dutch in Java. So Raffles was censured and told to confine his activities to the routine business of Bencoolen.

But a man of genius cannot be kept down. If you confine him in one direction he breaks out in another. Raffles was determined that British interests in the Islands should not be eclipsed and he appealed in a masterly despatch to Lord Hastings, the new Governor-General of India, against the disastrous view of the Cabinet. Hastings was not a small-minded man. Raffles' wide vision fired his imagination and in 1818 he invited him to Calcutta.

45

INDIA HOUSE, LONDON : THE SALE ROOM
Aquatint from Ackermann's *Microcosm of London,* 1808

To the Marquess, Raffles explained what had long been in his mind. From Bencoolen it would be impossible to cope adequately with the Dutch. A new British post must be found, not on Dutch territory but yet in the strategic centre of their island group, some position that commanded the straits of Malacca, the waterway to China. There was such a place. The Dutch had overlooked it. It was a small island at the extreme tip of the Malay peninsula, where once had stood the ancient city of Singapura. The island belonged to the Sultan of Johore. If he were induced to sell it, a city could be built there which, ideally situated both for trade and defence, would assure British commerce throughout the Far East.

Raffles had an irresistible way with him and the Marquess was fascinated. " Sir Stamford, you may depend upon me," were his last words as he speeded him on his way to Singapore. The negotiations with the Sultan of Johore were carried through rapidly and at the beginning of 1819 the British flag was hoisted on the island.

Then the storm broke. When the Dutch heard that the Englishman they feared more than anyone else in the East had broken from his Elba at Bencoolen

46

and found an unguarded spot inside the fence they had striven so hard to make impenetrable round their preserve, they were furious. For a moment it looked like war. It was rumoured they would sail in and take Singapore, which was garrisoned by a mere handful of soldiers under a Major. The Directors in London quailed. That incorrigible Raffles! Why had they allowed him to go East a second time? Why had they not long ago recalled him to England? The Foreign Office heartily shared their opinion. Raffles' action might plunge all Europe into war! Lord Hastings received several very nasty letters, but though the authorities in London expressed their displeasure in the plainest terms, they were afraid in the end to overrule their Governor-General and left the matter to his discretion.

But Hastings to his eternal glory stood by Raffles. He did not believe the Dutch would fight and airily declared that " we could but expect that in the event of our securing a station which would baffle the injurious policy of our neighbours, they would not fail to impugn our right to take possession."

He was right. The Dutch did not fight. The storm blew over. In 1824 Bencoolen was ceded to them on their recognizing Singapore. The place had become a city almost in a night. In the first year its population reached 5,000 ; by 1824 it was 30,000. The foundations of the citadel, upon which the defence of India and of Australia was to depend, had been well and truly laid. Nay, more, by a twist of fate it would be to that same strong place that a hundred and seventeen years later the Dutch themselves would look for the protection of their Island Empire.

When he had accomplished this his crowning work, the full significance of which is only now in this year 1941 fully revealed to us, Raffles prepared to return home. But some power was jealous of his immortal fame and dealt him blow after cruel blow. First, three of his children suddenly died, and he with his wife fell gravely ill. When he did set out, the ship went on fire and he lost all his property, including his immense oriental collections. After he was settled near London, the India House basely demanded £22,000 from him on account of salary paid in excess many years before. And three months later, aged only 45, he fell dead of apoplexy.

GOVERNMENT HOUSE AND COUNCIL CHAMBERS, MADRAS
Aquatint by H. Merke, 1807

# TABLE OF CONTENTS AND LIST OF AUTHORITIES